REACHING FOR THE RIM
BOOK 2

REACHING FOR THE RIM
BOOK 2

BILL ALEXSON
with
Stephen Andrulonis

THOMAS NELSON PUBLISHERS
Nashville

Library of Congress Cataloging-in-Publication Data
(Revised for volume 2)

Reaching for the rim.

"A sportswitness book."
Vol. 1 lacks volume designation.
Vol. 2 compiled by Bill Alexson and Stephen
Andrulonis.
Summary: Basketball players describe their
Christian commitments and how it has influenced their
lives and professional careers.
1. Basketball players—United States—Biography—
Juvenile literature. 2. Basketball players.
3. Christian life. I. Alexson, Bill. II. Hill, Terry.
III. Andrulonis, Stephen.
GV884.A1R43 1987   796.32'3'0922 [B]   87-7715

Library of Congress Cataloging-in-Publication Data

ISBN 0-8407-77758-2 (pbk. : v. 1)
ISBN 0-8407-73151-5 (v. 2)

Published in Nashville, Tennessee, by Thomas Nelson, Inc., and distributed
in Canada by Lawson Falle, Ltd., Cambridge, Ontario.

Scripture quotations are from the NEW KING JAMES VERSION of the
Bible. Copyright © 1979, 1980, 1982, Thomas Nelson, Inc., Publishers.

Printed in the United States of America
2 3 4 5 6 7 - 95 94 93 92 91

Dedication

To all those gifted men who so willingly shared their personal stories;

To all the young people and not-so-young people who look up to the professional athlete as a "Super Hero";

To the chaplains who faithfully minister, knowing all too well that "Superman" really is Clark Kent;

To the "Greatest Coach" that ever lived and the Only One who can give real meaning and purpose to life far beyond the game or the fame.

CONTENTS

Rolando Blackman
Dallas Mavericks
95

Kevin Duckworth
Portland Trailblazers
99

Mark Price
Cleveland Cavaliers
103

REACHING FOR THE RIM
BOOK 2

KEVIN JOHNSON

Phoenix Suns

Guard

The people who influenced my athletic career were Julius Erving and Steve Garvey. Now that's a strange combination.

I admired Dr. J. because of the way he handled himself off the court. He really was admired more for what he represented off the court than for some of the things he accomplished on it. And we know why Julius carried himself the way he did—because he was a Christian and was representing Christ. As for Steve Garvey, people used to say that the worst thing about him was that he was too nice.

I played college ball at the University of California and I was picked fairly high—No. 7—in the NBA draft in 1987. I spent half of my first season with the Cleveland Cavaliers and then was traded to Phoenix where my career has taken off.

In my first season I came off the bench fairly

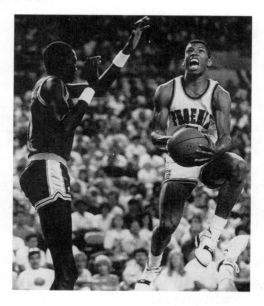

often and averaged just a little better than nine points a game. My second season I played more and more and averaged twenty points per game. After the season I was named the most improved player in the NBA. That's been the highlight of my career so far.

I started searching after Christ when I was a senior in high school. I began reading books by some of the great thinkers of human history. I studied the works of Henry David Thoreau, Ralph Waldo Emerson, and Plato. Life didn't add up for me. It didn't seem fair and I thought these men would explain it. Finally, as a junior in college, I really sat down and read the entire New Testament. A bit later I began attending church regularly. I decided this was the example to follow; Christ was the man above men. So I made a choice to live for Him.

Almost immediately my thoughts and desires began to change. I developed a sincere desire to read the Bible. I really wanted to know more about Christ. All the things I used to consider exciting—parties, chasing women, etc.—were no longer that exciting to me. The Truth, the Word of God began to excite me. He really changed my attitudes.

He can change your attitudes too. Just come to Him and recognize His salvation and His love for you. Sooner or later you have to be who you are; you have to be your own man or woman. You can run with the crowd and be influenced by what it does. But you are unique and you won't always have those people around you, telling you how to think and act. Dare to be different now. Stand up for yourself and make some right choices. The best choice is to choose Christ and take Him as your Savior. Do that and you'll find that you'll never be the same.

After that, practice your Christianity. Get into the Bible and get into church.

On the court, make the sacrifice to practice if you plan to be the best you can be. The players who are with me now in the NBA are the cream of the crop. But we all started out with a love for the game and a desire to be the best.

TERRY CUMMINGS

San Antonio Spurs

Forward

I grew up in the inner city of Chicago in a rough public housing project named Cabrini Green. For many young people, the neighborhood determines what they will be when they grow up. I can tell you that it doesn't have to be that way.

In my early teens, there were a lot of police cars and jail cells for me. But at sixteen all that changed. I knew there had to be a major turnaround. I had heard about Jesus Christ and what He would do for me if I accepted Him into my life. I knew this was a commitment I had to make. Many people had told me about Christ, but I had to accept Him on my own.

This decision really caused some problems for many of my friends. One of them told me he had heard I had become a Christian, but there was no

way God was going to forgive me for all the things I had done. That really bothered me until I read in God's Word that He *would* forgive me, regardless of what I had done, if I would only ask Him. Wow, what a promise, especially to a mean kid like me! Apparently, this friend had only heard about the wrath of God, not the mercy and love He also has for us.

I had a pretty good high school basketball career and several scholarship offers for college. After I graduated from Carver High School in 1979, I decided to stay close to home and play for Coach Ray Meyer at DePaul University. During my three years at DePaul, we posted a 79–6 record. I guess some think we were a failure as a team because we never got past the first round of the NCAA tournament. I know now, however, that I learned more by not making it than I would've if we had won. It really helped to build character in my life, because I couldn't lose confidence in my ability based on one game. Sure I hate to lose, but consistency is what makes good ballplayers and is what got us to the tournament to begin with.

The San Diego Clippers chose me in the first round (second overall behind James Worthy) of the draft. I was named Rookie of the Year in 1983 and ranked tenth in the league in both scoring (23.7) and rebounding (10.6). I was the first rookie since Kareem Abdul-Jabbar to rank in the top ten as a rookie.

The Clippers traded me to the Milwaukee Bucks in 1984, and that's where I've been ever since. In my first two seasons with the Bucks, I averaged 21.7 points per game and 8.8 rebounds per game in the regular season. In 1985–86 I had 28 double doubles (double figures in points and rebounding), and I reached the 7,000-point plateau in the final game of 1986.

Athletically, I can't pinpoint any one major influence on my basketball career. I get my human inspiration from people who have overcome adversity or problems, people who take charge of their circumstances and keep moving toward their goals despite the difficulties. That always inspires me to give my best in whatever I'm doing.

On the other hand, when I see someone stop short of a goal and quit, that inspires me, too, because it reminds me that I have to finish what I start.

I speak to many teens about Christ and how He can make them successful in whatever He wants them to do in life. At each of these meetings I have the same theme: "I have the power to be what Christ wants me to be and more." With Him, I can be all the things He wants me to be. If I think He wants me to do something and I apply myself with the right attitudes in discipline, desire, and persistence, I can achieve it.

My best game in the NBA came against Philadelphia in the 1986 play-offs. That night I knew I needed to score more points than my average. Our team needed a lift, and I felt God wanted me to provide it for that game. I scored 41 points against a talented young player named Charles Barkley, and we won the game. God doesn't say you're always going to win the game, but He does say He'll help you to do your best. If you win, great, and if you lose, that's OK, too, if you've given all you have to give.

This philosophy doesn't apply only to athletics. If you know God wants you to be something, apply yourself to achieving it. I've learned that knowing what God wants you to do in your life is like having a road map to get to a place you've never been before. Without Him, you'll never know where you're supposed to go or how to get there. If you're in school, study your hardest. If you're involved in sports, play and learn your hardest there too.

One of my favorite stories in the Bible is where Peter saw Jesus walking on the water and wanted to walk on the water too. Peter asked Jesus to let him walk on the water, and Jesus told him to do it. Peter got out of the boat and was walking just fine—until he took his eyes off Jesus. Then he started to sink with all kinds of doubts and fears. To me the water represents the circumstances we encounter every day in our lives. What we have to do is keep looking at Jesus, no matter what the problem, and say "I'm going to walk on it anyway." Then do it.

In sports you have many ups and downs, and nobody likes problems. But when you have a personal relationship with Christ, and He's involved in your life on a daily basis, you can walk on anything.

SIDNEY MONCRIEF

Milwaukee Bucks

Guard

It took me a long time to come to know Jesus Christ and His salvation. I grew up in and around Little Rock and East Little Rock, Arkansas, where my family had one main house rule—if you went to school, you went to church. So I heard the gospel and learned about God from the time I was about five or six years old.

But I really didn't become a Christian until 1987. When my wife rededicated herself to God, I decided to find out what God wanted for my life.

Growing up in Arkansas I was a real big football fan; it was my first love. That's the way it is with many people in Arkansas. Once I developed my skills as a basketball player, though, I determined to make a career in the NBA.

I have enjoyed a lot of great moments in the

NBA with the Milwaukee Bucks. I have had some big years as a scorer and we've played in many play-off games. Every pro player likes to be in those money situations, those pressure situations in which a loss means you go home.

The athlete I've really patterned myself after is Julius Erving. Dr. J. handled himself with such grace on and off the court. He was a spectacular player, a champion, and a gentleman. He also is a Christian. Now that's the complete package, if you ask me. If you're looking for a guide on how to behave as an athlete, read about Julius Erving and study the story of his life.

Now after I became a full-fledged Christian, that is, one who really believes in Christ as the

Savior, I went through a gradual change in my life. There wasn't a big bang; my life wasn't radically altered. In comparison to some people, my life seemed pretty good. Inwardly, though, Christ made me brand new.

Since then, I've grown up as a believer. God's taught me the importance of hearing and obeying His Word and the importance of love. Love is revealed as a powerful force in the Bible. Think about it. Love drove Jesus, a perfect human being, to die for humanity. Love was His motivation. The more you love Him, the more He reveals Himself to you.

There are so many things trying to push you this way or that way. Take this simple word of advice: Learn about Jesus and pattern your actions after His. That's a big order, but it can be done if you focus in, work hard, and ask Him to lead the way.

DARRELL GRIFFITH

Utah Jazz

Guard

Let me start off by telling you that one of the greatest highlights of my life was graduating on time with my class in 1980 at the University of Louisville. I majored in communications and managed to maintain better than a "B" average in college. I wanted to tell you that because much of the news you hear about college basketball concerns players who don't go to class and who get free rides through school. It wasn't that way with me at Louisville.

Why? Well, for one reason I was from Louisville. I grew up there and was committed to helping my local team. I wanted to make the hometown folks proud of me for more than just my basketball skills.

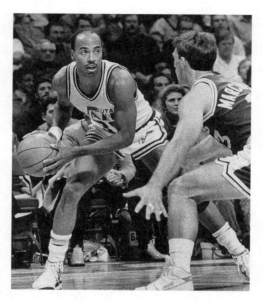

On the court I've had a lot of success. I was Mr. Basketball of Kentucky my last two years of high school. I was the first high school player invited to an Olympic tryout in 1976. I was an All-American my last two years in college. At Louisville, we won the 1980 NCAA championship my senior season, and I was the No. 2 pick in the NBA's draft in 1980 by the Utah Jazz. Then I set NBA records for three-point shooting when I hit 91 and 92 such shots in 1983–84 and 1984–85.

As I said, I grew up in Louisville and I received a rugged basketball education from my brother, who coached my YMCA team. Really, I always played basketball. I was on about four or five teams.

My family was very active in the Fifth Street Baptist Church in Louisville, and that's where I came to know Christ in the fourth grade. I was a member of the choir and I even sang lead on a couple of songs. I've never really strayed far from Him. At various times I've gone through adversity and He's been there for me. And in the good times I've been very careful to recognize Him and realize that He's been behind it all. As I've matured I've found that the Bible remains the most interesting book I've ever read.

One time when Christ really put my faith to the test came in 1985 when I broke my foot. I happened to be a free agent. The injury put my career into perspective. Many, many players are very insecure in their abilities and they rush back to the team. I took my time and really let myself heal, and as a result I've had three strong seasons since then.

From watching young people today I get the feeling that many of you are in a rush to grow up. Your peers demand that you act older than you really are. You have to have those high-priced tennis shoes on your feet just to make an impression. Realize this: ultimately the only one you will have to impress is God.

The thing to do would be to get started on that right now. Other people won't be there when the moment comes for you to face Him.

On the court, learn to work hard. Only the hardest workers are on the NBA teams right now. You won't make it there without hard work.

DEREK SMITH

Philadelphia 76ers

Guard-Forward

Think you've had it bad? My family and I didn't live in a home with indoor plumbing until 1981, when I was twenty-one years old and a junior in college. The house where I grew up in Hogansville, Georgia, consisted of four rooms—a kitchen, a living room, and two all-purpose rooms. We slept, played, and did just about everything else in those all-purpose rooms. Many of the kids I knew growing up had one goal in mind: to graduate from high school and land a job in the local rubber mill.

I was blessed. Basketball took me out of Hogansville and has taken me to places like Tokyo and Budapest, Hungary. I had two influences on my life in basketball. The first was my sister who was a very good basketball player and got me interested. My high school coach, John Penman, also really influenced me. He was a very disci-

Photography by Mike Maicher

plined guy who taught me how to play my game and how to stick with it.

The highlight of my basketball career had to have been in 1980 when I played on a national championship team at the University of Louisville. We were No. 1 and all of my family and friends could witness what was happening on television.

During my NBA career I have traveled all over. I've spent time in Oakland–San Francisco with Golden State and I've played with Sacramento, the Los Angeles Clippers, and now I'm here in Philadelphia.

I enjoyed a couple of very good years with the Clippers in the early eighties, but then my career was put in jeopardy by a knee injury and a bout with mononucleosis in 1985. That was the crisis point of my life. It also marks the moment I came to know Jesus Christ. It seemed like basketball was about to be taken from me, and I had to find something that would last. In my childhood I heard the gospel. I remember a preacher saying that when it was all said and done, God would be the one to carry you through. I decided at that time that I wanted to become a part of God's Hall of Fame. Forget the basketball Hall of Fame, I told myself. I contacted a friend, went to his church, and became a Christian that very day.

This was a very big change for me. I was known as "The Rock," someone whose emotions were always in control. *I* was always in control. But now I turned over control of my life to another—Christ.

One practical change in my life has been in how I view today. I always thought of what I would accomplish tomorrow. Now, I'm a day-to-day person. I know tomorrow may never be mine, so I make the most of the moment. I no longer take for granted the ability to run and jump and breathe.

Also, I've stopped listening to what men say. There was a point in my life when there was a five million dollar contract on the table and everyone came to talk to Derek Smith. Suddenly I had a knee injury and no one wanted Derek Smith anymore. Take note: men's opinions are very changeable.

My advice to you as a young person would be this: Don't choose to excuse yourself. Make your decisions and don't blame what happened in your past for who you are. Christ can bring you out of where you are and into the opportunities awaiting you. Learn to set your mind on Him and you'll never waver about what it is you must do.

Some basketball advice: develop into a two-sided player. The players in this league don't have a weak hand. If you're naturally left-handed, work on the right side. If you're a righty, work the left side. Become a fundamentally balanced and developed player.

JOE DUMARS

Detroit Pistons

Guard

I blazed a new trail in my family. Before me, the youngest of seven children (six boys), every Dumars was a football player—one of my brothers spent a season in the United States Football League.

I decided to set my own path. I thought I could be different if I played basketball. The town I was raised in, Natchitoches, Louisiana, just outside Shreveport, was a small one, but one filled with good athletes. The competition at Central High School was pretty intense. You felt like you had to push yourself or someone would catch up to you. Those early days probably instilled in me a desire to excel at what I did. My father told me to pick a sport and do my best. That's what I did.

One of the brightest moments in my athletic career came when I signed to attend McNeese State University in Lake Charles, Louisiana.

Photography by Einstein Photo

Going to college may not seem like a big deal to some people, but to a kid from a small town it was a tremendous accomplishment, especially since I was going to school on a basketball scholarship.

My last season at McNeese I averaged twenty-five points a game and was a second-team All-American selection. That was a great moment because just before my senior year I suffered a broken foot and was expected to be out for most of the season. But my mother and I prayed, and I came back to the team in six-and-a-half weeks.

That was a real miracle.

The Detroit Pistons drafted me in the first round—I was the eighteenth player picked—in 1985. Since coming into the NBA I have enjoyed a lot of success. In 1989 my team, the Pistons, achieved the ultimate as we swept the Lakers in four games to take the NBA Championship. To top it all off, I was named the Most Valuable Player of the play-offs.

I've achieved a great deal in my few years in the NBA. The important thing I've kept in mind is that I'm part of a team. I never set out to win a game by myself. During the 1989 season the Pistons came together and worked toward the title. Winning it was the culmination of all of our efforts.

Similarly, my coming to Christ at the age of fourteen was the culmination of the efforts of my parents. I was raised in an environment where Christ was preached. In our home we had parents who stood for Christ. I don't think I would have come to Him outside of that atmosphere.

After seeing my mom and dad live this way, I decided that was the path I wanted to take one night at a revival meeting at our church. It's not a story of a miraculous sign. The truth I was hearing from the preacher lined up with what I was seeing lived out in my home. It all came together in Joe Dumars's mind and I became a Christian.

I am tremendously thankful for what Christ is to my life. It seems very odd that people can get sucked into certain life-styles, but there is confusion when you don't have Christ. One thing Christ has done for me is let me see things for what they really are. I don't recognize gray areas; I see things in black and white. Every situation you experience, every choice you make carries a consequence. Either you draw closer to Christ or you pull away from Him. Really, that's all there is to it.

Let me give one hint about your game: Don't let yourself hear the people who put you down. Don't let it in, because doubt can creep in and make you ineffective.

STEVE COLTER

Washington Bullets

Guard

My dad encouraged me to pursue a career in basketball. And I think he was the best basketball player I have ever seen. He never did get to go to college and show what he could really do. You see, my dad was one of fifteen children, and he had to go to work to help support the family when he was a teenager.

But my father was allowed to go to the park on weekends. And there in that park in Phoenix, there was no better player. He could score at will. I used to watch him and dream about playing like him. Now here I am in the NBA.

Another thing I learned from my parents was the Christian way of life. They were both very active and remain active in the local church we attended in Phoenix. I was always a very inquisitive youngster and asked a lot of questions about what I heard in church. My mother would just tell

Photography by Mitchell Layton

me to search the things out for myself in the Bible. I accepted Him when I was about eight years old.

God has really kept me from a lot of things that might have prevented a career in basketball. In my neighborhood everything was available—cocaine, pot, heroin, and sex. I knew boys who had become fathers at age fourteen.

I was watchful, I examined things closely, and I saw the consequences of those things. Christ within me told me it wasn't right to get into those things. The consequences really were very clear to me. I stayed away from it all because I wanted to reach my career goals.

I did reach those goals after four solid seasons at New Mexico State University; I was drafted by the

Portland Trailblazers. Not long into the season, I had two big scoring nights back-to-back. In the first game I scored thirty-five points in about twenty minutes of play. The next game, I put in twenty-five. I really thought I was on my way to being a star. Instead, I've bounced around the league. I was in Chicago for a half-season, then I was traded to Philadelphia. I had a real good stretch of sixteen games and helped the 76ers make the play-offs that year. I came back the next season, and fifteen games into it, I was waived from the team.

I really had to look to God during the next twelve days, which seemed like four years. It was a tough time, but God really taught me about His faithfulness. I am now with the Washington Bullets. I'm still a reserve player, coming off of the bench, but I've learned to handle some difficulties. I know my day will come. I'll be ready when the coach calls me.

I couldn't do what I'm doing if I didn't have God with me. The pressure of wanting to be the star would really get to me. I pray, stay in the Word, and God keeps me ready. I'll make my contribution; God will see to it that I do.

Let me give you an athletic tip: Never watch the ball on the dribble. Learn to pass and shoot and to keep your head up so you can see the whole court.

TRENT TUCKER

New York Knicks

Guard

I didn't grow up in a tough family environment, so I don't have any stories about how I fought my way out of difficult situations and into the NBA.

My home situation was probably better than most because my family put God first and for that I'm very thankful. Now this is going to sound strange, but God used basketball to get me into church and ultimately into His family.

I was born in Tarboro, North Carolina, but grew up in Flint, Michigan. In Flint I wanted to play with this church league basketball team. One of the requirements was that the players had to be members of the church. So I accepted Christ, joined the church, and joined the team.

See, God can use anything, even a little orange ball, to get through to you. I'm not sure I really understood what was happening to me at the time I asked Christ into my heart, but God faithfully

revealed Himself to me through the Bible later when I was in college at the University of Minnesota.

I don't remember any one major incident. It's just that I slowly came to understand that God really was there for me. I thought on that more and more, and I thought more about the promises in His Word. I began to feel real peace of mind. There was a security I felt knowing God was there, backing me up, supporting me.

All of this really came in handy in my second year in the NBA. Let me set the scene for you. I came out of Minnesota after leading my team to the Big 10 conference championship. I was drafted in the first round in 1982 as the No. 6 pick by the

New York Knicks. That means the professional basketball people thought only five college graduates that year were more talented than I was.

My first year, I enjoyed some reasonable success for a rookie. I played in seventy-eight games, grabbed 216 rebounds, and averaged a little more than eight points a game.

The next season, I didn't play as much. I had to keep the faith. God's peace really ruled my heart at that point. He comforted me and let me know that He wasn't going to do anything I couldn't handle. As a result, I maintained my intensity, I stayed ready, and I delivered when I was called on.

In the play-offs that season I managed to win a couple of games with some big shots. I learned at that time that He knew what He was doing. Won't you learn that too?

My advice to you in these times of stress is to do what I've learned to do—put God first. If you can learn that, then the negative influences and pressures will be easier to withstand. Learn all you can about God by reading His Word. If you come to understand what He is really like, then you'll be more likely to call on Him when you need Him.

Athletically, I encourage you to develop the jump shot. Tuck your elbow in, concentrate on the hoop. It's the one shot college and pro scouts are really looking for in today's players.

CRAIG EHLO

Cleveland Cavaliers

Guard

You may laugh when I tell you this, but my mother was probably my biggest athletic influence. She was the basketball player in the family. She played in high school and she still had a mighty fine left-handed jump shot when she used to play against me.

I was raised in cattle country, down in Lubbock, Texas, with two older sisters. We were a very close family and church activities were always deemed important.

There weren't any athletes I really looked up to; I just played all the sports. Except football, that is. I was kind of small and got beat up in that game. I finally settled on basketball when I was about ten, I guess. I started working hard on perfecting my skills.

After I finished high school no college really showed any interest in me as a basketball player. I

wasn't recruited at all and I resigned myself to getting my education at Texas Tech there in Lubbock. I figured I was pretty much through as a basketball player when I received a call from the coach at Odessa Junior College in Odessa, Texas. I spent two seasons there, went on to Washington State, and then was drafted by the Houston Rockets in the third round in 1983.

With the Rockets, I experienced my greatest thrill as a professional so far—playing in the 1986 NBA Championship Finals against the Boston Celtics. Maybe you remember me. I was the guy who made the slam dunk right at the end of game number six as hordes of Boston fans rushed the court to celebrate the Celtics's victory.

I'm a Christian because of basketball, and there's a little story about how I came to know Christ. In the fall of 1986 the Rockets released me. About three months after that, Mark Price went down with appendicitis and I got a call from the Cleveland Cavaliers. I enjoyed a good run with the Cavaliers and wound up sticking with the team even after Mark healed up.

Months later, in November 1987, I attended a Bible study at Mark Price's house. He asked me point-blank if I knew where I would wind up if I died at that moment. I didn't know. Mark then explained to me how Christ conquered death through His resurrection and told me how I could receive and have assurance that I would go to heaven.

I accepted Christ that moment, and I was changed. My tongue changed. My marriage and my career shot up like a balloon. Statistics no longer meant that much to me. I used to tear the newspaper open to the scoreboard page to see how I did in comparison with some other guys. All of that is gone now. I play my game and I play it hard.

I made a choice that night at Mark Price's home. You need to make choices too. But learn to make informed choices. I made my choice because of the truth Mark told me. Get advice. Seek out older people and older athletes and coaches and learn from them. Accept the advice and learn from it. Then, put it into action.

STEVE ALFORD

Dallas Mavericks

Guard

Allow me to make a point here at the beginning. The player I patterned myself after was Jerry Sichting, a 6-foot-1 guard who played for my father when he coached at Martinsville High in Indiana. I took Jerry as my example because I figured I would wind up being about his size with similar abilities. The problem for many young players is that they set their sights too high—that is, you idolize players who are way beyond what you will be in physical abilities. I knew I would be a guard. So I concentrated on becoming a guard.

I've told you that my father was a high school basketball coach so you know that I was around the game all my life. My parents had everything to do with my interest in basketball. Even my mother, after being married to a coach for so long, could tell me things about the game.

As a player and a Christian I've been blessed. In

1983 I was Mr. Basketball of Indiana, and then in 1987 I helped Indiana University win the national championship. In 1984 I played on the U.S. team when it won the gold medal in the Olympics at Los Angeles.

Probably my biggest disappointment came in high school. I wanted to take my dad's team to a state championship and wasn't able to do it. That was an ultimate goal of mine and it didn't work out. It was a very bitter experience to play my last game for my father and not have it be for the state championship.

My home life was very Christ-centered, and I was taught Christian values from birth. Just before my junior year in high school, I finally was mature enough to understand what it meant to ask Christ into my life. Since then I've followed Him by concentrating on the Word of God. I've learned to lean on the Lord at all times. I've also learned that you don't always grow the way you would like. You sometimes take steps backward; you maybe put God on a shelf for a few days. It takes concentration to follow Him. More importantly, I have found you need a willingness to come to Him when you've struggled or failed.

I've really come to appreciate God in the good times. Knowing Him makes the good times that much better. God's been very faithful to encourage and motivate me to be the best I can be. I don't pray for a big, successful career. I do ask Him for peace of mind and ask Him to use me for His purposes.

I know my upbringing is very different from what some of you are experiencing. I haven't faced some of the obstacles and confrontations that you do every day. Still, I can say this: Christ makes the difference in your life. No one cares for you like Jesus.

As a basketball player, fall in love with the game and just play, play, play.

ALEX ENGLISH

Denver Nuggets

Forward

I guess you could say I've been running with a crowd all of my life. I grew up with thirteen kids—brothers, sisters, cousins—in a tightly knit family in Columbia, South Carolina.

There wasn't a male figure around to be a role model for all of us, so my grandmother took it upon herself to be the head of the household. And she did a wonderful job. The most important thing she taught us was that God was first in our lives. She made Him first in our household.

That was the seed of my belief in God and Jesus Christ. Many of us are fortunate to have that seed planted early in our lives; some of us are not so fortunate. But there's always time to come to Christ. He's always waiting for you.

From that early seed we can grow. It just took a long time for that seed to take root in my life. I finally accepted Christ in 1983 at a Sports Power

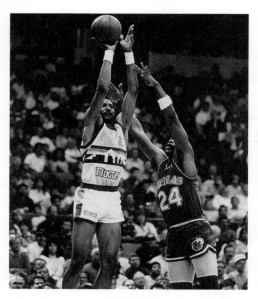

Ministries pro basketball conference in Hilton Head, South Carolina. It was one of the most beautiful times in my life.

On the athletic side of my life, I was a big fan of Bill Russell and the Boston Celtics. Bill Russell was always the underdog, but he always ended up the winner. He couldn't jump that high, he wasn't 7 feet tall, but he won championships. He worked hard and he knew the details of the game of basketball. Around the basket there was no one better at getting in place for the rebound. Another thing about Bill Russell was that he never let himself get down after a bad play. He just kept doing his job.

The bad things pass, the mistakes pass; the ups,

the downs, they all pass. With faith in Christ you have the strength to carry on. Remember this: a bad play or a bad game is a very, very small thing in the big picture God has created.

My goal was to make the All-Star team and I finally did. But after becoming an all-star I realized there were more important things to consider. So one year I remember we got organized and all of the players donated their All-Star money to a fund set up to help those starving in Ethiopia. We, the players, managed to raise $125,000. The NBA team owners matched that total and we could send off $250,000 to help needy people.

My desire to help people has come from knowing Christ.

Put your faith in the Lord and maintain a tunnel vision toward Him and the positive things in your life. Be determined to have a goal. As a shooter you work on your concentration. You learn to zero in on the hoop and let the ball fly. Do the same thing with Christ.

Zero in and let yourself fly.

MYCHAL THOMPSON

L.A. Lakers

Center

I'm going to say something that may surprise you: Muhammad Ali was one of the biggest influences on me as an athlete. That may sound strange because I'm a basketball player and he made his mark as a heavyweight boxer.

I always admired Ali for his devotion to his religion, even when he was very wealthy and successful. And he was willing to do something that caused a lot of misunderstanding and criticism—he changed his name. Ali was willing to identify himself with the god of Islam. I don't think his religion is the right way. Obviously Jesus is the answer. But I believe many Christians are afraid to admit they belong to Christ, even though they believe the truth of the gospel.

Another thing I respected about Muhammad Ali

was the way he could back up everything he said. He came off as a loudmouth, but he made good on what he said.

God makes good on what He says too. His Word is full of great promises, and all are true. I took Him up on one of those promises at age eleven. I received Christ into my heart, and He's given me strength to follow Him and live for Him ever since.

I grew up in the Bahamas and coming to Jesus didn't seem like a big deal at that time in my life. My home was a real Christian home. Christ was taught to me from the time I was in the cradle. The transition was easy because it just seemed like the only way to live.

I have enjoyed a number of highlights in my

athletic career. In 1977 I came out of the University of Minnesota and was drafted No. 1 by the Portland Trailblazers. What pressure that put on me right away! My career has had me moving around the league a couple of times. But I finally landed with the Los Angeles Lakers three seasons ago and with them I have enjoyed some of my greatest moments as our team won two straight NBA championships.

There have been tough times in my career, but I choose not to dwell on those. In fact, I refuse to refer to those times as low lights. They really weren't low lights; they were times when I needed to learn, to mature, and to grow as a person in Christ. I look back and I see God's purposes in those situations. He's made me an overcomer.

Being a professional athlete can be a struggle for a young person. The money you receive is tremendous. There are pressures, however. People desire to influence you this way and that way. Do yourself a favor and learn now to avoid bad influences. Develop self-respect and stand up to those who would like to involve you in drugs and other harmful things.

Take a look at those you know who are involved in drugs. Are they successful? They might be right now, but it won't last. That kind of life-style leads to dependency and burnout. Simply, they've lost all control. I should say they have given up control. Taking drugs is a choice.

Do you want to be a good athlete? Learn to make good choices. Convince yourself that practice makes perfect and never let yourself get tired of it. Talk to someone about a supervised weight-lifting program and be serious with it. This kind of training can prevent injuries later on. Develop team skills like passing and offensive rebounding and setting screens and picks. And talk to winners. Get to know people who are team players and understand what it takes to win.

You can apply those same principles to your Christian life. Develop the practice of prayer and Bible study and keep at it. And get involved with winning Christians—people who serve God down deep. You can spot the phonies. You know who believe in Christ on the surface but only serve Him when it's convenient.

JON SUNDVOLD

Miami Heat

Guard

I considered myself one of the fortunate ones. When I was growing up, I was part of a small-town Christian family that was always involved in church and the community.

And I had a father who devoted a lot of time to me and my three brothers. He didn't spend his free time out on the golf course or trying to make more and more money. My dad liked to be with us. He was always playing catch or shooting hoops with us. It was great.

But more than that, I had a father who pointed the way to the heavenly Father, God. See what I mean! I was fortunate. Some people travel long and winding roads to Christ; I was born into a family that loved God. Being raised in a Christian home put the fear of God in me; it kept me on the straight and narrow.

Still, I made choices for myself. In high school

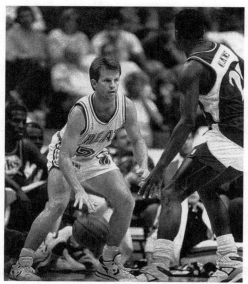

South Florida Images

and college I started searching. I asked myself, "What is Christianity?" and "Who is Christ?" I had accepted Christ as my Savior early in my life. Later, I studied the Bible and found out for myself what it was really all about.

I didn't fully realize how important all of this was until I came to the NBA out of the University of Missouri in 1983. At Missouri I played all four years on the varsity and my number (20) was retired after I finished my college career.

The Seattle Supersonics made me a first-round selection in the draft that year, and I had a solid season for a rookie, with 239 assists and a 6.9 scoring average. I also made my first twenty-five free throws that season.

I was to spend only one more year in Seattle, however. I was traded to the San Antonio Spurs before the 1985 season. That's one of the difficulties of being a professional athlete. You don't control where you're going to play from one year to the next. I wasn't needed in Seattle and I was traded away.

Playing basketball for a living was like a dream for me, but professional sports can be like a roller coaster ride. For a while it was difficult, and I understood that I had to get back to Christ and lean on Him a little more than I had been. Since then every step in my career has brought me to a better place for me and my family. Following the 1987–88 basketball season, the Miami Heat acquired me in the expansion draft. Another move, but it wasn't a big deal. I knew Christ would be with me in Miami as He had been with me in Seattle and San Antonio.

It's no surprise where I am today because Christ brought me to this place.

I love the people in the NBA. That's my highlight: the friendships I've made and hope to keep after I've left the league. I don't glory in my personal accomplishments; the people I have met and worked with are what I cherish.

But even with all the people I've met, I've held to one firm principle: being true to myself. Remember that, please—always remember that you have to answer to yourself. Friends and peers may influence you, but you go home each night and face yourself and God.

Grow in Christ. You'll find He brings out the best in you.

KIKI VANDEWEGHE

New York Knicks

Forward

Perhaps you'll envy me when I tell you that I grew up in the bright lights and big city atmosphere of Los Angeles. Even in the midst of all of the glitter, my family were down-to-earth, church-going folks. I was introduced to the gospel of Christ at an early age. I was raised in an environment that made it easy for me to learn about the Lord.

As a kid, I wasn't pushed toward this sport or that sport. My parents encouraged me to try all the sports. Eventually, I settled on basketball. And I really worked. I'm still known as one of the biggest gym rats in all of L.A. I mean I was always found somewhere shooting hoops. So it's no accident that I have a nice shot today.

I've got one of the better shots in the NBA, and

I've been fortunate to be a pretty good scorer throughout my career. Every team likes a player who gets them points. So God has blessed me in that regard.

Overall, my NBA experience has been extremely positive. I've made the All-Star team a couple of times. Also, I've been injured a few times. Being on the sidelines is the pits. You are a great competitor or you wouldn't be playing sports. And to not be able to play really eats at you.

My greatest highlight in sports came in 1980 when I made the academic All-American team and helped UCLA to the national championship game. My team lost to the University of Louisville with Darrell Griffith, but it was a real thrill because we weren't expected to do anything that season and we came up just one game short of the national title.

Another great highlight was my coming to the chapel program while with the Denver Nuggets. It helped to have someone come and give a message from the Bible. The life of a professional athlete features plenty of long airplane rides and mad dashes through airports. These messages really kept me going.

Now I always look at each situation in life as a 2-on-1 fast break with me and the Lord on the same team. You can't lose in those cases. Anytime I have a problem with a decision, I just ask Him for direction. In a quiet moment, He's always faithful to answer and give strength. As a Christian, each of us has a direct connection to God. At any moment, we can get guidance from Him and from His Word. If you practice these things, I think you'll find yourself very fulfilled. You won't need some of the things that are being offered to you such as drugs, alcohol, sex.

As an athletic tip, there are so many knowledge-able coaches available today. Get with one of them and ask him to critique your game. Then go out and work on the problem areas.

MARK ACRES

Orlando Magic

Forward

You may think you have it bad. But man, I grew up with parents who were both teachers. Try getting away with something in a household like that. (I'm only kidding.) I'm very thankful for the environment that my parents raised me in. It was a Christian home. We loved the Lord. Christ's name was spoken often in my home, and it still is.

About basketball, my father taught me all I know. He coached me at Palos Verdes Estates High School in California. He also coached me later at Oral Roberts University.

My career has taken me across the country and overseas. I've spent seasons in Belgium and Italy. And I've played with the Boston Celtics. That first season, I played on a team that went to the NBA finals. That stands out as one of my greatest thrills as a professional player.

But my greatest thrill in sports came very early

in my life. When I was six years old, I played on a soccer team that wound up with a California state championship for our age group. I'll always remember the feeling of being a champion. As a Christian, I should always feel like a champion. Jesus conquered sin and death on the Cross and at His Resurrection. The best part about it is He did it all for us. It's free. We can come to God and He'll give us the gift of life. That's a tremendous promise.

At the age of seven, I came to know Christ as my Savior. Evangelist Billy Graham spoke at a stadium near us and my mother thought it would be a good idea for the family to take the opportunity to hear his message. Tom Landry, the former coach of the Dallas Cowboys football team, also was on hand. Their messages got through to me, and I went forward to receive the Lord as my Savior.

Since then, I have come to understand that the Bible has so many things to say about how you live your life. You have God there all the time. I need Christ every game. I'm 6 feet 11 inches and 225 pounds, but I need help. I need the peace He brings to my heart in order to play effectively.

Each of us faces choices every day and we need to make the right ones. If we do, we'll draw closer and closer to the Lord. Discipline yourself to think with God, to have thoughts that are in line with His Word.

Also, learn the fundamentals of your sport. Think about what makes a good jump shooter, a good rebounder. Did you know most rebounds are taken under the rim? Always make the effort to block out your man and get in the proper position near the hoop.

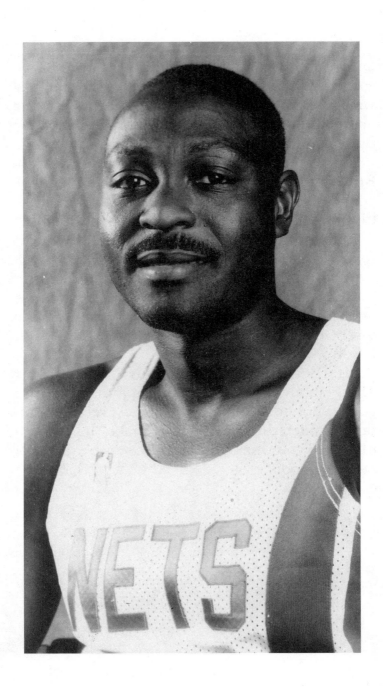

PURVIS SHORT

New Jersey Nets

Forward

I was raised in the small town of Hattiesburg, Mississippi. We were pretty tough all the years I was growing up. But there was one constant: church. Mom always made sure we were in church every Sunday. When you're small you don't understand the value of such consistency. But now that I think back about it, I'm so thankful for the way my mother did things.

In high school, I started to consider what God wanted of me. I gave my life to Him and He helped me to become a strong basketball player. I knew that I had to win a scholarship to college because my family didn't have the money to send me there. I discovered at that time that He always was there to care for me. I finally won a scholarship to Jackson State University in Jackson, Mississippi.

Basketball was in my blood, I guess you could say. My brother Eugene spent a season with the

New York Knicks back in 1975. So I had him to learn from. Also, I watched Oscar Robertson, the great guard with the Cincinnati Royals and the Milwaukee Bucks. On the court he was so disciplined. He was always thinking about where to put the ball. He knew who to get it to.

Off the court, the man many of us admired was Julius Erving. The way he carried himself made for a good example. Every athlete should pattern themselves after the classy Dr. J.

I've enjoyed twelve solid seasons in the NBA, and that's something I thank God for every day. Back in 1986, I injured my knee and thought that my basketball skills were gone for good. It wasn't just a sprain, it was a torn ligament. The message I took out of all of that was that there was never a time to take things for granted. It was tough coming back. Rehabilitation became a real strain; there were times when I couldn't stand the pain.

About that same time, a pastor who was a very close friend of mine was hit by a car. He spent many days in the hospital, and I spent a lot of time there, too, talking and praying with him. Those days changed the way I looked at life. I came to understand that prayers really are answered and that the Bible is a great book of comfort and hope.

Let me give you something to take out on the court with you. There are four points to remember about shooting: you must have good balance; you must focus in on a spot on the basket; keep that elbow tucked in. And follow through with your shots.

BUCK WILLIAMS

Portland Trailblazers

Forward

I look back on my youth with great delight. I enjoyed y days as a child growing up in Rocky Mount, North Carolina. My mother brought up me and my two brothers and two sisters as Christians.

Early in my basketball career, I watched Kareem Abdul Jabbar closest of all. He was graceful and tough for a big man. I wanted to play the game with his intensity and style. Off the court, I've done my best to pattern my life after Christ.

I played college ball at the University of Maryland and then was drafted third in the 1981 NBA draft. The first eight years of my career I spent with the New Jersey Nets and there were some good times. In 1984, we staged a marvelous upset of the Philadelphia 76ers in the first round of the play-offs and shocked the sports world.

But in 1988–89, the Nets struggled through a

very tough season. The team won only twenty-six games. Still I tried to keep my game together. Some guys asked me why I still played hard for a team going nowhere at the time. I admit it was very frustrating to play under those circumstances.

Yet, when you believe God, you know things will come out all right. I prayed and trusted Him to put me where He wanted me. After that very trying season, I was traded to Portland and I enjoyed one of my greatest seasons. The fans were coming out and we were among the very top teams in the league. God had a plan in it all, just as He had a plan for my salvation.

My best friend growing up was a guy named

Wesley Johnson. His mother was a very giving, caring person, someone you wanted to be around. She introduced Jesus to me and I accepted Him.

All this time, it's been so good to have Christ there for me to look up to. He's been everything, though I can't really describe it. As a young person, you have to know who you are in Christ. You have to determine to be a pioneer and not a follower. Those who follow are often led into trouble. Learn to be led by the One who has your whole future in front of Him at once. The God of grace wants to make you something very special. Please believe it and give your life over to Him.

As a ballplayer, develop an attitude that every ball that comes off of the rim is yours and go after it.

ROLANDO BLACKMAN

Dallas Mavericks

Guard

I was fortunate to have a man like Ted Gustus around when I was growing up in New York City. He's now the coach at Nazareth High in New York, but back then he always hung around my neighborhood. What was he doing? Giving himself to the kids. He was important to me because my dad left home when I was eleven and Ted was sort of my substitute dad.

He was interested in me as a total person, too, not just as a basketball player. He was religious and we all responded to his kindness and love. Without his being around, I'm not sure what would have happened in my life. I may not have developed the discipline necessary to become a good ballplayer, capable of playing in the NBA.

I played high-school basketball at William

Grandy High in New York, and then I went on to
Kansas State University. My first year away from
home was really rough and I almost withdrew
from K-State and contemplated a move back to
New York and St. John's University. God was
really with me at that point. I didn't go back home
to the old neighborhood crowd. I stayed at Kansas
State and hit a thrilling shot at the buzzer to win
an NCAA tournament game against Oregon State
in 1981. I went on to be named an All-American
that same year.

After college my perception of basketball
changed. That first year in the NBA was rough.
Nothing is guaranteed at the professional level.
You hear teams call themselves a family, but pro

sports is all business. If you don't do the job, you're out of a job. That realization hit me hard. Basketball had been so easy, so much fun up to that point. Now it was work. The perform-or-else ideal really shocks a young player.

After two years of struggling through the pressure of this game on my own, I recognized that I really needed to depend on the Lord more. I had received Christ as a youngster and back then my mother told me to stick with Him through good and bad times. This was a bad time, so I went to Him. Suddenly life didn't seem so complex to me. The gray areas were gone. Now my basic approach to life is to rest in God. I keep things simple, I follow the Bible and do what it says to do.

In basketball, learn to keep things simple too. Forget all the fanciness and learn to do all of the skills well. If you aren't a complete player, you haven't made it. As a shooter, lock in on the rim. Pick a spot, focus, and fire.

KEVIN DUCKWORTH

Portland Trailblazers

Center

Don't give up. I'm a testimony to what can happen if you don't quit. Way back at Thornbridge High in Dolton, Illinois, I was a slow starter. I was always big—I'm 7 feet tall and 280 pounds now—but still I was cut from the varsity team as a freshman. Did I give up? No. I worked on my game, especially in the summer, and made myself a better player. I played more and more through my high school years and really blossomed as a senior.

I landed a scholarship to Eastern Illinois University and my pattern held. That first year I played only part-time and managed to average around 10 points a game. As a senior in college, I again blossomed, averaging nearly 20 points and pulling down 290 rebounds in 32 games.

Things didn't change once I arrived in the NBA. My first season with San Antonio and Portland, I played very little and averaged just 5 points per game. Everything changed the next season as I won the NBA's Most Improved Player Award. Now, I'm a regular and I'm with a good strong team.

I always stayed ready—that was my secret. I never took sitting on the bench for granted. It wasn't where I wanted to be. I worked on my game and when the time came for me to go in, I ran in and made an impact. I wanted to do my best for the glory of God.

You know, the worst time in my career came in 1987–1988 season when I tried to play for people.

You can't please people. Even the best of fans can get down on you sometimes. Jesus didn't try to please people and neither should you. People are fickle, so if you try to please them, you may become only confused or defeated. When I was younger, for example, everyone told me I was too fat to play basketball. Now look at me. I put things in God's hands and I managed to get invited to several NBA tryout camps. There I was noticed and made a career in the pros.

Give everything to God and commit yourself to Him. Love people. Respect people. Honor people. But do things for the glory of God, not for the praise of people.

You have so much to offer, and God has a special plan for you. Stay away from the materialistic traps of this life. Learn what God wants you to do and do it with all your strength. Whether you're a pastor or a pro basketball player, God really wants to use you. We all have a purpose.

Remember, players are made during the summer. The work you put in during the off-season is what will make you strong during the regular season. Also, remember that the smart guy gets the rebound. Use that body and put yourself between the man and the ball.

MARK PRICE

Cleveland Cavaliers

Guard

Not many people get to make a living doing something they thoroughly love like playing a game. Realistically, I never thought I would play in the NBA. Yes, I had a lot of honors in high school and college, but those things don't cut it when you're on the court with the best basketball players in the world. They could care less how good you *used* to be.

Since I'm the son of a basketball coach, I guess you could say I had to play the game or else, but Dad never forced me to. Dad used to coach in the NBA and now coaches at Phillips University, a small college in Enid, Oklahoma. He always encouraged me and my two brothers in all sports, but I knew basketball was to be my main game. I made the All-State team and was a high school All-American.

Growing up in a Christian home meant a lot to

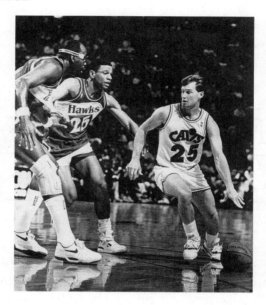

me. It helped me to keep my priorities straight and put athletics where they should be. Our family was very musical, and I even sang in a gospel quartet with my dad and brothers, while my mother played the piano for us.

Several colleges recruited me, but Georgia Tech in Atlanta stood out in my mind. Their coach, Bobby Cremins, was just beginning to get their basketball program back on the map. They were also in the Atlantic Coast Conference, the toughest basketball league in the country. By choosing to be a Yellow Jacket, I was on the ground floor of building a winning tradition at a school known mainly for football. So after graduation from Enid High School in 1982, I headed off to Atlanta.

I had a pretty successful four years at Tech, where I majored in management. We didn't win the NCAA national championship, but we played in the tournament and once in the NIT. I finished my college career as the tenth all-time leading scorer in Atlantic Coast Conference history. I was also the only freshman ever to lead the ACC in scoring, which I did in 1983. I was named an All-American as a sophomore, junior, and senior, and MVP of the ACC Tournament in 1985. Georgia Tech won its first regular season title ever that year, and we missed going to the Final Four by just one game when we lost to Georgetown.

I was drafted in the second round (twenty-fifth overall) in the 1986 draft by the Dallas Mavericks. They traded me before the season started to the Cleveland Cavaliers. I play for them now. Winning the ACC, being the MVP in the ACC, and playing in the NBA are things few people attain or even have a chance to try for. The feelings that came along with those events were just great. But I can honestly say that none of it compares to having a personal relationship with Jesus Christ. My commitment to Christ didn't start until my senior year in high school. I was at a youth revival at my church when I knew it was my time to give my whole life to Christ. Since that time, my life hasn't been easy, but He's always there to bring me through when it's tough. Even when things are going great, I have to give Him the credit.

I married my college sweetheart, Laura, on Christmas Eve in 1986. Our honeymoon was real short since I had a game to play in Cleveland the next day. It meant something extra special, however, to be married and start my family on the same day we celebrate Jesus' birthday.

To be a good basketball player, you have to be committed to doing the best you can. You must start with the fundamentals—dribbling, shooting, passing, and defense—and practice more than you want to. I remember that on Friday nights as a young person, when all my friends were getting ready to go out and have fun, I was getting ready to have my fun down at the gym. I wasn't forcing myself to play, but I just loved basketball and couldn't get enough of it. I think that's the key. If you love basketball and really enjoy playing it, and if you keep it in the right place behind your relationship with God, your family, and your studies, you'll become the best basketball player you can possibly be.

SPORTSPOWER MINISTRIES

Sportspower Ministries has celebrated ten years of bringing God's message of love and forgiveness to the pro athletes of America and the youth who look up to them. Founded and directed by Bill Alexson, Sportspower Ministries works alongside other ministries to counsel and teach the pros through Bible studies, pregame chapels, and conferences.

Sportspower Ministries has the privilege to send pro athletes worldwide to conduct clinics and speak in schools and churches, sharing their personal stories and their commitment to Christ.

For more information about Sportspower Ministries and speaking requests, write to:

SPORTSPOWER MINISTRIES
P.O. Box 404
Perry Hall, MD 21128

STEPS TO A PERSONAL RELATIONSHIP WITH GOD

Each of these players has spoken of a personal relationship with Jesus Christ. If you desire to have this personal relationship too, just do the following:

Believe:

• God loves you and has a specific purpose for your life.

• Sin (unbelief) keeps you from knowing Him.

• Jesus Christ died on the cross for your sin so you can know Him personally.

• You must invite Jesus Christ to come into your life and be your personal Savior.

Pray:

"Dear Lord Jesus, I need you. I acknowledge that I am a sinner, but I thank You for making full payment for my sins when you died for me on the cross. As of this moment, I accept You as my personal Savior and ask you to come into my life."

If you have just believed on Christ today, the Bible declares that you are a child of God (John

1:12)! Eternal life is now yours as a gift. For more information about growing in your new personal relationship with Jesus Christ, please write to:

Sportspower Ministries, Inc.
P.O. Box 18715
Baltimore, MD 21206

ABOUT THE AUTHOR

Bill Alexson is the founder and executive director of Sportspower Ministries and the founder of the Player's Chapel Program to the National Basketball Association. As the chaplain to the Boston Celtics and former Professional Basketball Player in Europe, and for Athletes in Action, a division of Campus Crusade for Christ, Bill Alexson is well aware of the highs and lows of the athlete in the spotlight.

Bill speaks internationally, thus fulfilling his desire to see the youth across America and the world reached with the powerful testimonies of these well-known heroes.

Along with his wife, Valerie, and their son, Brandon, the Alexsons reside in White Marsh, Maryland, where they are actively involved in full-time ministry.